# SUITED & BOOTED

# SUITED *&* BOOTED

FROM SHARP SUITS TO THE PERFECT SHAVE:
A MAN'S GUIDE TO LOOKING GREAT

PAUL COPPERWAITE
**photography by** KRISTIN PERERS **styling by** ALEX LEWIS

RYLAND
PETERS
& SMALL
LONDON NEW YORK

Design & Art direction *Pamela Daniels*
Senior editors *Miriam Hyslop*
 *& Catherine Osborne*
Location research *Jess Walton*
Production *Gordana Simakovic*
Publishing director *Alison Starling*

Styling *Alex Lewis*
Text *Paul Copperwaite*

First published in Great Britain
in 2007 by Ryland Peters & Small
20–21 Jockey's Fields
London WC1R 4BW
www.rylandpeters.com

ISBN-13: 978-1-84597-505-0
A CIP record for this
book is available
from the British Library.
Printed in China

While every care has been taken in
researching and compiling information
in this book, it is in no way intended to
replace or supersede professional
medical advice. Neither the author or
the publisher may be held responsible
for any action or claim howsoever
resulting from the use of this book or
any information contained in it.

# contents

## style
8

## accessories
26

## grooming
40

## Originality is Nothing New

There used to be a time when any self-respecting man would not have answered the door without attaching a collar to his shirt. These days, in your leisure hours, you're free to wear what you like – clothing that's comfortable, what would have once quaintly been called bohemian. And in some areas of the media or entertainment, where it pays to be an individual, the same rules may apply to your working hours.

We've become so good at being funky that we may need a few pointers when it comes to elegance. Sir John Birt, as BBC Director General, reportedly derided the wearing of neckties. Meanwhile, designer Hedi Slimane, now at Dior, was pioneering the return of post-punk skinny ties to the catwalk and street. Now that dressing down, once rebellious, has become an orthodoxy, we've even fewer places to turn to for style advice.

You don't need an excuse like a party or wedding to dress up. You're free to look stylish any time. We shouldn't let casual culture encourage us to think of formal clothes as less comfortable. The made-to-measure style of bespoke tailoring should guide our purchases, even of ready-to-wear suits. In fact, a suit that's more elegantly form-hugging will be more comfortable, and will bring out the best in its wearer. Comfort is an essential part of the right look, whatever your shape.

If you're feeling good about your job, don't let your appearance send out a different message – your suits should reflect your confidence. As Slimane says, 'I'd like to think there's a return to elegance, a revival of the notion of fashion for men. I've mounted a crusade against this informal "casual Friday" trend. I'd like men to think about evolving into something more sophisticated, more seductive.'

STYLE

## CLASSIC STYLES:
### Suits you, Sir

If you make the right purchasing decisions, you can look good in a suit whatever your body shape.

• The shoulders are especially important – **thin men** look best in a narrow cut with little or no shoulder padding, narrow trousers, slim lapels and a nipped-in waist. The jacket should fall softly over the hips.

• A **broad-shouldered**, athletic type should similarly go without shoulder padding, but with a more flattering double-breasted outfit.

• A more **corpulent man** should avoid features that

make him look larger. Lapels of a medium width are more suitable. Whereas slightly shorter trousers, with their hem at Achilles tendon rather than heel, will lengthen the look of the legs. Belts have a tendency to bisect the body laterally and shorten its appearance, but braces will elongate it.

## SIGNS OF A GOOD SUIT

- Although a matter of design rather than quality, it's usual for the shoulders to have a slight slope.
- The first one or two of the sleeve buttons can be undone.
- Trousers sit high on the hips and are close-fitting to the legs.
- Traditional British jackets have two side vents, one on either side. A three-button jacket can have one at the back, but a double-breasted jacket should always have two side vents.
- Typical of custom-made suits is a loop behind and below the buttonhole on the left lapel.

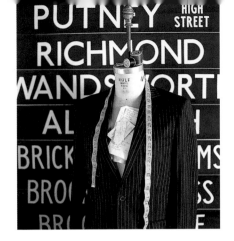

## BESPOKE, MADE TO MEASURE, OR DESIGNER READY-TO-WEAR?

The tailors of London's Savile Row and its neighbouring streets include famous names such as Gieves & Hawkes, as well as smaller premises where the tailors are effectively cutters who contract out the tailoring for a bespoke suit (adapted to your particulars from a typical set of measurements). Some men happily spend four figures on a designer suit without realizing that for similar money, if they are prepared to wait for their product, they can purchase one from such a tailor.

# BRITISH STYLE:
## Evolution not Revolution

The suits that we consider formal work attire today were only introduced to offices in the 1930s. Before that, clerks, scriveners and their superiors wore morning jacket, waistcoat and trousers of differing materials. British design remains steeped in tradition, with an emphasis on looking appropriate. Despite this, the British relish the challenge of bending the rules; breaking them is a little too easy.

Your choice of suit should 'suit' the occasion, the time of day, and the time of year. There are three aspects to this:

### CUT

- **Single-breasted two-piece** (most popular choice). This is available with two or three buttons, a centre vent at the back of the jacket or two side vents. Trousers may or may not have turn-ups.
- **Double-breasted**. Two side vents or, unusually, sometimes none, but never just one.

- **Three-piece**. Although rendered unnecessary by central heating, the waistcoat is making something of a comeback, both as part of a suit with retro charm (Gieves & Hawkes offer them) or as a stand-alone fashion item.

### COLOUR

- Traditional business colours are black, dark blue, and dark to light grey. Lighter greys are currently becoming more fashionable.
- Green or brown (especially a tweed suit) are best reserved for classic sporting events, leisure or self-consciously hidebound work such as academia or antiques dealing.

### FABRIC

- There are many weights of material, and you should think about the temperature in which you'll wear your suit before buying. Medium weight is recommended for year-round use.
- As the most crease-resistant natural fibre, wool is still the best option.

• Popular fabrics for business include:
plain worsted in all colours and weights;
white (or blue) pinstripe on blue; grey
pinstripe; chalk-stripe on grey; and 'nailhead',
a more discreet pattern in blue or grey.

# AMERICAN STYLE:
## United Tastes

From Wall Street to the Grand Canyon, the USA is a vast and majestic country. Americans have created clothes to deal with the highest corporate corridors, and the great outdoors, both as unforgiving of the underdressed in their different ways.

From snap-brimmed postwar style, through Ralph Lauren's preppy look to Tom Ford's glitzy populism, sartorial America has simultaneously stated both its individuality and its homogeneity, in which all members of the world's most ethnically diverse population can proclaim themselves American with ease.

Contrary to European impressions, America has strict traditions of dress, particularly on the East Coast. How else could they have given us the concept of 'dress-down Friday'? For formal business-wear, in addition to European patterns (see pages 12, 16), Americans favour grey flannel or herringbone and Prince of Wales check – traditional leisure-suit fabrics in Britain. In summer, light blue or beige suits make an appearance.

Diasporas brought many Jewish and Italian tailors to the USA, while clothes from Madison Avenue's Brooks Brothers have been worn by Abraham Lincoln and many significant Americans since. Their classic 'sack' suit is the model for many formal designs, with a single vent and a three-button jacket. The top button is ironed into the lapel and not used. Jackets may be available in up to five lengths – the longest of which is surprisingly 'zooty' – with sloping shoulders that give a more casual silhouette. Trousers aren't usually pleated, and the waistbands sit high on the hips.

Perhaps the most formal/semi-formal exported American item is a shirt with a soft-roll collar (see pages 34 & 35) based on John C. Brooks' design. They may or may not be button-down, and are available plain, or in plaid or stripes for casual wear.

# ITALIAN STYLE: La Dolce Vita

In the 1950s, Italian fashion brought glamour back to the world of the suit. Italian style entered America via Hollywood, with matinée idols such as Gary Cooper and Clark Gable sporting Italian tailoring, and the clean-cut cool of Gregory Peck in *Roman Holiday*.

There are two good reasons for the appeal of Italian style: design flair that meets the demands of the catwalk season, and a tradition of using light materials (on account of Italy's dry climate) that ensures you'll be cool during the summer season. Merino wool, cashmere and even mohair can feel lighter than a typical shirt, and suits can be half-lined to ensure shape while letting body heat dissipate. Italy also pioneered the use of cotton and linen.

Traditional suits from tailors based in Rome, Milan or Naples are aspirational products. Among the cognoscenti, names such as Brioni, Kiton, Caraceni, D'Avenza and Cifonelli are unmistakable for their cut, rather than their label. A fitting at one of their premises is desired by financiers and gangsters alike.

From the 1980s, Italian ready-to-wear brands brought individuality to the manufactured suit, again via Hollywood. Giorgio Armani in particular has moved from the pushed-back sleeves of Miami Vice to monochromatic sharpness. Dolce & Gabbana, together with others such as Ferragamo, continue to combine exquisiteness with new references and, in Versace's case, a knowing vulgarity that incorporates rock and street features – such as patched jeans – into couture.

In the tradition of the *passeggiata*, in which one demonstrates one's self-worth, Italian designers have taught us to see clothes as creating an opportunity for self-expression.

ITALIAN DESIGNERS *have taught* US TO SEE CLOTHES
AS CREATING AN OPPORTUNITY FOR *self-expression.*

# HOW TO WEAR A DINNER JACKET (without being mistaken for a waiter)

Although 'white tie' invitations have tailed off for all but the most specific events, you would have to adopt a very alternative lifestyle to avoid wearing a dinner jacket (also known as a tuxedo) on occasion. Jackets may be single- or double-breasted, in black, midnight blue or white (usually for open-air events), with silk-trimmed lapels or a shawl collar. Trousers should sport a plain silk braid, and no turn-ups.

Tuxedos are an expensive investment for infrequent use. Second-hand examples may require a little alteration, otherwise you can personalize a well-fitted suit on hire.
- 'Black tie' will mean just that in Europe, but Americans accept some variety. White belongs with tails.
- Wear a cummerbund that matches your tie, with the pleats facing upwards. There used to be a pocket hidden in the pleats to hold opera or theatre tickets (hence the tradition of pleats facing upwards).
- A white linen or red silk handkerchief will look great.
- Black silk knee-length socks are traditional, ideally with patent leather dress shoes (or Oxfords).
- Cuff links are essential, in black and/or gold. Shirt studs may be available to match.
- A tux needs a white dress shirt, bib reinforced with cotton piqué or pleats finishing well above the waistband.

## TIE YOUR OWN BOW TIE
- Adjust tie to your size.
- Cross left over right at narrow area, loop it behind and pull into a simple knot.
- Fold the end now on the left in half at the widest part. You'll recognize one half of the bow-tie shape. Hold it in place.
- Place right end over narrow part of left. Bring it underneath. Repeat the loop.
- Fold right side at widest point and pass through loop. Pull carefully.
- Tighten, holding both folded and open ends on either side.

# A GREY AREA

When it comes to street fashion, anything goes. Look funky, feel sexy, or just blend in; it's up to you. For work, we adhere to a dress code, or select clothes that make us look successful. So what do we grab from our wardrobe when an invite states smart casual?

The phrase strikes a doubtful note with anyone who's had a weekend invitation to meet the boss's partner. These are the times when it's easy to stumble into being underdressed or overdressed.

Christopher Bailey, creative director at Burberry says, 'If you feel you're overdressed, you're probably really overdressed.' Think of the time of day, the time of year and whether you will be indoors or al fresco. During the day a suit may be too much. That goes equally for informal events outdoors, with the honourable exception of a classic tweed suit at a racecourse of course.

The market has mushroomed, however, with trendier, form-hugging leisure suits for wearing past cocktail hour. To judge by Dolce & Gabbana and Armani, monochrome is in. Black, much touted, may be severe, but grey has come full-circle. Once the staple colour of wintry flannel trousers worn with a sports jacket, in a leisure suit it suggests the effortless style of Gregory Peck or the Rat Pack.

If the occasion is quite conservative, there are classic combinations such as tattersall check with corduroys, or preppy chinos with a blue jacket (if not quite the full blazer of Ralph Lauren's look). Otherwise:

- Always wear a shirt rather than a T-shirt.
- Pinstripe jackets with jeans are a fashion statement of the past.
- A busy shirt – with stripes or a pattern – is fine with jeans or chinos but suits are better with plain shirts.
- Lambswool or cashmere sweaters are classic in reds and blues and fashionable if thin, patterned and short.

# SPORTS & STYLE

Many style touches have practical origins – jackets have vents so that we can sit comfortably without feeling restricted, and to allow us to put our hands in our pockets. And nothing places more practical demands on our clothing than sports.

If you think of sportswear as style, street fashions come to mind. The surfing, snowboarding and skate wear now available from British labels and seen throughout suburbia, for example, was inspired by the need for total freedom of movement. The bright, protective second skins of racing motorcyclists have spilled on and off catwalks

for years and now the traditional plainer jacket of the street biker – the Belstaff – is the new Barbour (itself a shooting garment) for aspiring supermodels. Then there's the ubiquitous baseball cap. Perhaps the best way to adopt this is with a plain suede model such as by Mexx.

## THE SPORTING LIFE

*   ***English country pursuits*** have given us tattersall check shirts in cotton and wool, coarse tweed suits – single-vent, three-button – riding macs, the hacking jacket (the original sports jacket, cut for horse riding), moleskin and cord trousers.
*   ***Golf*** has popularized polo shirts, windcheaters,

check trousers and of course the golfing umbrella.
*   ***Tennis*** has given us Lacoste – the hardy perennial to smart-casual that Fred Perry is to street wear. René Lacoste was himself a tennis pro and 'Le Croc' his nickname.
*   ***Landlubbers*** everywhere 'sport' Henri Lloyd, a blue blazer, boat shoes, the more typically British Guernsey pullover, which all originated for the yachtsman.

DAMPENING A SHIRT *with a spray bottle* AND PUTTING IT INSIDE A PLASTIC BAG FOR TWENTY MINUTES *ensures it's evenly damp.*

*One should 'rest'* A PAIR OF SHOES FOR A DAY *after a day's wear.*

# STYLE KNOW-HOW

## TAILORS' TLC

- Good suit hangers have shaped shoulders and a trouser hanger with a clamp that holds the bottom hem so trousers regain shape under their own weight.
- Air your suit for a while before putting it away, perhaps near an open window.
- Invest in a good clothes brush. Don't brush too vigorously.
- Hanging your suit in a steam-filled bathroom will remove creases.
- Invest in a trouser press, or iron your trousers with a damp white cotton cloth between them and your iron.

## IRONING – HOT TIPS

- Dampening a shirt with a spray bottle and putting it inside a plastic bag for twenty minutes ensures it's evenly damp.
- Begin with the sleeves, in the centre, and rotate outwards, ironing the creases last.
- Iron a button cuff button-upward. Open up a double cuff and iron it completely smooth. Fold and iron, then line up the folded cuff and iron at the top of the cuff.
- Preserve the back pleat by ironing it along the edge of the board.
- Open the collar and iron it from the tips inward to avoid creases. Iron both sides, with collar-stiffeners still removed. There is no need to iron it folded.

## SHOE CARE

Handmade leather shoes accrue far less odour than man-made materials. With re-soling as required, they can last as long as you do, moulding to your foot and acquiring a patina that's the opposite of box-fresh.

- Scuff new leather soles with a wire brush to improve grip.
- Allow mud to dry, then remove it with a stiff bristle brush.
- Polish with a horsehair shoe brush and colour-appropriate wax polish. Finish by buffing with a duster.
- One should 'rest' a pair of shoes for a day after a day's wear.
- If you don't have shoe-trees, stuff shoes tightly with newspaper for storing.

# ACCESSORIES

*It's easy to overlook the importance of shoes:*
GIVEN THEIR POTENTIAL EXPENSE,
QUALITY FOOTWEAR CAN FEEL LIKE SNOB VALUE.

# BEST FOOT FORWARD

It's easy to overlook the importance of shoes: given their potential expense, quality footwear can seem like snob value. But a fine pair of shoes will lift the appearance of an average suit. As Guy West of bespoke manufacturer Jeffery West says, 'You can pick up a second-hand suit, accessorise with a pair of welted shoes, and fool a tailor.'

A pair of Oxfords or brogues from Church, Cheaney, Grenson or John Lobb should be snug and supportive but not tight. Buy from a retailer who conducts a proper fitting, including for width (indicated by a letter after your shoe size), such as Baber's in London's Oxford Street or Church's in Regent Street.

The most formal of traditional closed lacing shoes is the plain black Oxford, perfect for ceremonies or worn with a pinstripe suit. Shoes that feature a line of decoration across the toecap are less suitable for a Palace reception, but only just. Less formal still are half-brogues, with brogueing (patterning consisting of punched holes) on the toecap and uppers, and full brogues, or 'wingtips', where the pattern sweeps down the sides of the shoe to the heel. Full brogues match the widest variety of suits, including softer flannels or tweeds. Sharp, modern spins on classic welted footwear are available from J. P. Tod's, Jeffery West, Poste, Paul Smith and Patrick Cox.

Traditional casual shoes are available in brown or burgundy, suitable with autumnal colours and corduroys. Suede spins on a full brogue are common, either with rubber or crepe soles. For a less heavy shoe, try loafers such as a classic Church, or Bass's famous Weejun. Lighter still are moccasins such as J. P. Tod's or Gucci's 1980s classic. Chelsea boots suit a narrow trouser, while chukka boots are rediscovered winter-wear.

Classier trainer options include Sperry plimsolls or Jack Purcells by Converse, while trainer-style comfort can also be found in Rockport or Camper.

# LEARNING LUGGAGE

The world of air travel has given in to the practicality of the ubiquitous wheeled holdall in hard-shell or nylon. Although for many of us luggage is the last thing we'd expect to be stylish, it's possible to buy good quality items from manufacturers such as Samsonite and Tumy. For the shorter trip, carry the antidote if budget allows; a Keepall-style bag such as a Louis Vuitton (with its trademark toile Monogram) or a classic Gladstone bag such as Mulberry's. Over-the-shoulder suitbags don't store clothes as well as a traditional, horizontal suitcase, and should be stored in a hanging position whenever possible.

## WORLD OF LEATHER

A belt should not overpower a suit, even if you're snake-hipped, so leave the rock-god buckles to be worn with jeans. For formal wear, be elegantly waisted with a classic black or brown brass-buckled belt to match your shoes.

The traditional height of luxury is a tailored jacket with custom pockets. Failing that, it's still possible to carry your essentials without carrying a bag:

• A traditional rectangular wallet is less bulky than a squarer design when placed inside a suit jacket. A bulky wallet will also look unsightly in a rear trouser pocket. If you're going without a jacket, it's better to use a card-sized wallet that can slip inside a waist pocket. Some may like billfolds for notes while others find them Mafioso.

• Your mobile phone belongs in a pocket.

• Leather keyholders and change purses protect your pockets from wear.

## HOW TO PACK A SUITCASE
### (without creasing your jacket)

• Lay your jacket facing you in the bottom of the case.

• Lay your trousers along the crease and fold them inside the top half of your jacket, sideways to it.

• Insert rolled-up socks or underpants into the shoulders.

• Lay the sleeves across the chest and fold the bottom half over the top.

# THE POLITICS
# OF UNDERWEAR

**Boxers or briefs?** The chances are that, like most men, you'll have been confirmed in your answer to this ultimate question for some time. While many men experiment in their teens, they tend to come down on one or other side of the fence as time goes by.

In Britain, boxer shorts became the underwear of choice in the 1980s, partly helped by Nick Kamen's appearance in a famous Levi's advertisement, while briefs took on dull associations. In the past, tailors routinely made boxer shorts to measure, offering clients the choice of their shirt materials for a product ideally suited to the roomy trousers of a traditional British suit.

Today's boxer shorts, however, often tend to be made of thinner cotton or silk, with a tendency to ride up under lightweight trousers. What their fans consider freedom, others experience as a lack of protection.

The alternative, the Y-front, or Jockey brief, was first manufactured by Cooper of Wisconsin in 1934, and offered support that had previously only been available from the jockstrap (hence the name). The company itself would also later adopt the name Jockey. While some experience the style of this brief as restrictive, it's worth noting that authentic Y-fronts are elasticated more firmly around the outside of the thigh than the inside.

However, as is usual in politics, the question is more complicated than it first appears. In addition to the traditional Y-front, there's a wide choice of briefs designed to support and shape the male anatomy, with or without a fly, including Speedos and Jockey's own Poco Brief. Men who appreciate this aspect of briefs but prefer a little more cloth now have a third way – the A-front trunk. Introduced in the 1990s, these feature brief-style tailoring around the groin with legs that extend down the upper thigh – possibly offering the best of both worlds.

# SHIRTS & TIES

How to spot quality in a ready-to-wear formal shirt:

- Look for collar bones (unless it's soft by design, like the button-down shirt in the photograph opposite). These prevent the tips of the collar turning up.
- The sleeve is pleated where it meets the cuff. It's a bonus if the pattern/check lines up between the two.
- Quality shirts are longer at the back than the front.
- The more stitches a seam has, the better the quality – about 20 per inch on a good shirt.
- A triangular gusset is often sewn into the cutaway at each side. In Thomas Pink shirts for example, these gussets are trademark pink.

## COLLAR CHOICES

Turn-down collars are the business norm. The wider the distance between the collar tips, the more formal you will look. You should shorten the look of a long neck with a high collar; the opposite applies for a short neck. Brooks Brothers' soft-roll collars have a buttoned-down business look, but can also be dressed down. Current fashion favours longer cutaway collars, patterned, and grey or white shirts.

## TIES

The necktie persists thanks to business tradition and mod-style influences. Create contrast with a pocket handkerchief, or use a plain handkerchief as a feature when no tie is required. From British club ties to fashion ties, all good makes have features in common: three-part stitching (barely visible diagonal seams) and a good interlining. Good ties come in silk, fine cotton, cashmere, or other wool. Top-end makers include Tobias of Savile Row, Drake's, Hermès, Charvet and Marinella.

BROOKS BROTHERS' *soft-roll collars* GIVE A BUTTONED-DOWN BUSINESS LOOK, BUT CAN ALSO BE DRESSED DOWN *relatively easily.*

# EYEWEAR: wear your spectacles – don't let them wear you.

As recently as the 1980s, schoolboys who wore glasses were seen as geeky. Times have changed. Today, spectacles are trendy and draw on a vast range of styles and technological advances such as titanium frames and plastic lenses. Top fashion brands include Paul Smith, Marchon, Cartier, Tag Heuer, Gucci, Chanel, Mont Blanc, Dolce & Gabbana, and Dior. Top-notch opticians such as Cutler and Gross carry the widest selections.

Fashion moves between more imposing frames that state their presence boldly, and less assuming pairs that suggest discretion on the part of the wearer. It's important not to follow fashion to the point of obscuring your best features, or to choose frames that are wrong for the shape of your face.

You may be considering laser treatment or contact lenses (the better to wear your Ray Ban Wayfarers or pilot-style sunglasses), but specs still represent the easy option. Choose glasses that highlight your best feature – brown frames with brown eyes, for example. Frames should be to scale with your face, and contrast with its shape.

## THE SEVEN TYPES OF FACE

- **Square** – soften the angles and lengthen the face with narrow, rounded/oval styles, with more width than depth.
- **Round** – narrow, angular frames, wider than they're deep, will add length, as will arms that begin at the top of the lenses.
- **Oval** – wide, oval frames draw attention to your face's natural balance.
- **Rectangular** – a low bridge shortens the nose. Decorative frame features add width.
- **Diamond** – highlight eyes and cheekbones with rimless or curvilinear frames.
- **Base-up triangle** – (hairline wider than jaw) – widen the jawline with frames that are wider at the cheeks.
- **Base-down triangle** – (jaw wider than hairline) – widen the hairline with frames that are wider at the top.

# FULLY ACCESSORIZED

## COOL CUFFS

Cuff links add an extra spin to your shirt, tie and suit. Faced with the bewildering variety available, it helps to start conservatively – gold or silver, oval or round. Match with your jewellery and spectacles. It's also easy to pair up a wide range of single-colour ties and enamel links in commonly seen colour schemes – dark green, (wine) red, and dark blue. Shirtmakers will also provide fabric knots that enable you to cover every colour-combination in your wardrobe for a pocketful of small change.

The sky's the limit for precious metal or antique

cuff links. Some men have heirlooms from female relatives adapted to be worn as links. But 'costume'-priced ones are never sniffed at – they simply suggest you've left your expensive ones at home. Meanwhile, there's nothing sub-standard about a button cuff compared to a French cuff. American preppy shirts with a soft-roll collar have them, for example.

## BAND OF GOLD

When it comes to jewellery, you'll know your own taste and ultimately have your own style. Still, here's how it's traditionally done: wedding rings are plain bands of yellow or white gold, with a semi-circular cross-section, if embellished at all. Trinity rings, featuring three discreetly woven bands, are also tasteful. For more decorative rings, focus on the little finger of the left hand. If you want to sport more than one extra piece, focus on having more than one ring on your actual wedding finger.

## KNOWING THE TIME

The popularity of watches
shows no signs of waning –
it's simply easier to glance
discreetly at a watch than
at a phone or PDA! Despite
chunky fashions, a squarer
'dress' watch, such as
a Cartier or a Jaeger-
LeCoultre, suits thinner
wrists, while action-
men can carry off the
chronographic Breitlings,
Omegas and Rolex.

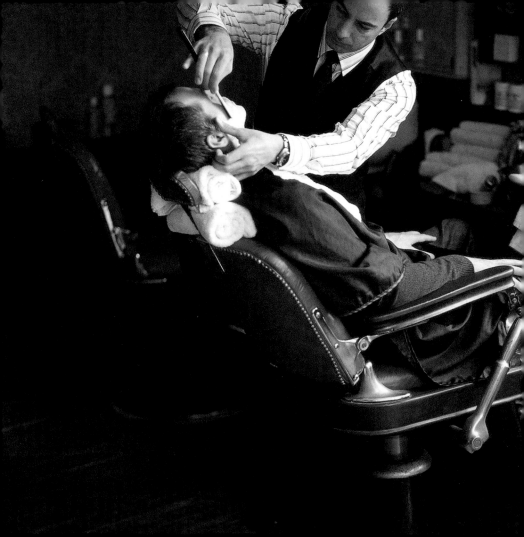

# GROOMING

## THE SKIN YOU'RE IN

Men's largest organ, the skin, is governed by testosterone. On average, male skin is a quarter as thick again as women's, and darker. As Tim Brown of Procter & Gamble Prestige Products (the company behind Hugo Boss' cosmetics) says, 'Across all skin types, male skin is darker than female skin. These might be evolutionary signals that we're not aware of, but a darker skin tone does seem to be a sign of masculinity.' Unfortunately, darker skin is also more acidic, and produces more sebum and collagen, than lighter skin.

Daily shaving adds to the trauma, causing dryness and skin sensitivity. Luckily there's an increasing arsenal of products for our protection. You don't have to buy in to all of them, but any of the following will do what they say on the tin!

## SHAVE IN LUXURY

• Beard hair can absorb twenty per cent of its weight in moisture and a pre-shave, such as ClarinsMen Shave Ease Oil, applied before the shower can soften it further.

• There are a number of shaving foams for sensitive skin, such as Biotherm, as well as gels from Nivea and Aramis. Otherwise, you'll get the longest lather from waxes and creams such as Molton Brown Ultracalm Lemon Leaf Shavewax, or those from Truefitt & Hill, Kiehl's or The Art of Shaving.

• Triple-bladed razors – or more – appear to lead to a higher incidence of in-growing beard hair than single- or double-headed shavers. Two seems to be the ideal number when it comes to multi-headed razors.

• A styptic pencil is an old favourite for staunching a shaving cut if you have to leave the house in a hurry. Before safety razors, they used to be essential to any shaving kit.

## FACE THE WORLD

- Throw away the carbolic. Normal acidic soap dries and ages the skin. Use a face wash instead. *Recommended*: Nivea, Neutrogena, or Men-Ü Ultra-Concentrate Healthy Facial Wash (contains tea tree oil to soothe shaving rash).
- Moisturize and exfoliate for a healthy skin. *Recommended:* Clinique Maximum Hydrator or Boss Skin Healthy Look are no-nonsense, while L'Oréal Men Expert and Prada Hydrating Gel Cream represent a bigger step in being tinted.
- Using a clay mask up to once a week may seem excessive, but can take years off your face. *Recommended:* Anthony Deep Pore Cleansing Clay.
- While anti-wrinkle cream has yet to conquer the men's room, quick-fix concealers are finding a market with men who like to stay up late and get to work on time, while less immediate anti-ageing treatments, are becoming more popular. *Recommended:* YSL's Touche Eclat, Dr. Andrew Weil for Origins' Mega-Mushroom Face Lotion.

## YOUR TYPE OF SKIN

It's important to know your skin type if you're going to indulge in more than one skincare product.

- *Normal* – neither oily nor dry, but soft, smooth and elastic. Follow a daily cleanse, tone and moisturize routine.
- *Dry* – flaky, dry, tight skin. Use nondetergent, neutral-pH products to cleanse your skin and moisturize daily. Avoid using commercial soap and hot water.
- *Oily* – usually thicker and firmer than normal skin, with larger pores that are prone to blackheads. Use a glycolic facial cleanser, followed by an astringent and oil-free lotion.
- *Combination* – usually has an oily 'T'-zone (forehead, nose and chin) with dry cheeks and eye areas. Use the skincare advice provided for both dry and oily skin.
- *Sensitive* – susceptible to damage from sun, wind and rain, often blotchy after shaving, sensitive skin can also be prone to allergic reaction. Avoid scrubs and use fragrance-free washes and moisturizers. Consult a dermatologist if problems persist.

# FRAGRANCE

Keep fresh with a deodorant, however be aware that most contain aluminium, which evidence suggests could lead to health problems. Aluminium-free products, such as L'Occitane Baux's deodorant stick, are a good alternative.

Aftershave is made by dissolving herbs and flowers in carbon disulfide or petroleum ether (benzine), which is then distilled. Anything derived from more traditional methods of *enfleurage* or, less floridly, the absorption process (such as *huile antique*) is a little more special. Some fashion brands still employ an in-house creator of scents, or 'nose', whose brief is to 'trick' our mind into making pleasant associations. As perfumer Jean-Claude Ellena of Hermès explains, 'It's an illusion!' Fragrances consist of head notes (the light, volatile scents you smell at first), and middle and base (or basic) notes, the 'bouquet'. Aftershave formulae replicate dry, masculine base notes such as leather, tobacco or wood.

## FRAGRANCE PHRASES:

*Eau de Cologne* – contains two to five per cent perfume oil in alcohol and water. Refreshing.
*Eau de Toilette* – a solution of four to 20 per cent perfume oil.
*Eau de Parfum* – 10 to 30 per cent perfume oil. Strong, more expensive.

## THE CHOICE:

Alongside masculine modern aftershaves, there are some timeless smells that go with a classic wardrobe:
*Acqua di Parma* – rose, fougère (fern with a floral top note).
*Davidoff or Knize Ten* – oakmoss oil (woody).
*Eau d'Hermès* – the original unisex perfume.
*Eau Sauvage* – oakmoss oil with a top note of citrus.
*Egoïste by Chanel* – vanilla.
*Polo/Polo Black by Ralph Lauren* – oakmoss oil, patchouli, fresh top note.
*Trumper's Extract of Limes* – typically English Eau de Toilette.
*Vetiver by Guerlain* – oakmoss oil, patchouli, fresh top note.

# NOT-TOO-WEIRD BEARDS

It's now considered acceptable to sport facial hair. Although a matter for your own taste, the trick is to keep it tidy enough to look intentional rather than unkempt.

A sharp suit and a goatee make a characterful contrast, much like a dark suit with a pair of Nikes. Be aware however that the more extreme the fashion statement, the more easily it dates (the ponytail and mullet are good examples of this). Stay ahead of the curve.

We know facial hair is time-saving, but it's also an ingenious solution for irritated skin (see pages 60 & 61). If you flirt with facial topiary, be sure to flatter the shape of your face. Grow a full beard before trimming along the following lines:

- *Old-school moustache* – doesn't help a weak jawline, but covers a thin top lip. Keep hairs straight with a wax such as Pinaud-Clubman or Stern.
- *Full beard* – allowed to fill out, it hides a thin face and, grown at the neck and trimmed on the face, a double chin. Tidy it with round-ended scissors and comb downwards with a beard comb or brush.
- *Under-lip triangle* – strengthens a weak jawline. Keep it trim.
- *Three-day stubble* – shave with a beard trimmer at around grade 1.5 every couple of days.
- *Defined lines* – requires a strong jawline and dark beard hair. Cut with razor and scissors or invest in a Philishave D-finer.
- *Goatee* – keep the outline shaped and hair short with a beard trimmer. This style suits a weak chin.

If you're just experimenting, 'own brand' beard trimmers are fine. However, for a more permanent 'installation', hairdressers recommend Wahl.

If you flirt with facial topiary, *be sure to flatter the shape of your face.*

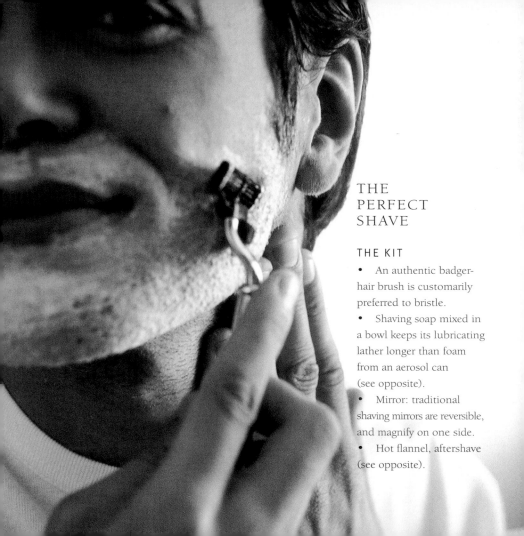

# THE
# PERFECT
# SHAVE

### THE KIT

- An authentic badger-hair brush is customarily preferred to bristle.
- Shaving soap mixed in a bowl keeps its lubricating lather longer than foam from an aerosol can (see opposite).
- Mirror: traditional shaving mirrors are reversible, and magnify on one side.
- Hot flannel, aftershave (see opposite).

- Razor: while many love the idea of perfecting the clean shave of a cut-throat razor, a non-lethal style requires practice. Multi-headed safety razors, such as Gillette's Mach 3 series, are more practical.

## THE SHAVE

**Before shaving**, a barber will wrap your face in a steamed towel. Soften your beard hairs in a similar way with a hot washcloth. After a shower is a good time to shave. Ideally, have a light source in front of you.

**Dip your brush into warm water** and apply emulsified shaving cream to your beard, lather the two and allow time for the hairs to soften. Don't let it become too dry.

**Shave your cheeks first** and draw the razor in the direction of your beard-hair's growth, or 'with the grain'.

**Raise your nose or cheek** to taughten the skin of your upper lip. Take care around your lips, on the point of your chin, and don't miss the area beneath your bottom lip unless you mean to.

**Rub off remaining soap** with a clean towel and pat dry. Job done!

# WHAT'S UP TOP?

Along with our clothes and shoes, our hair is a social signifier, but one that's less easy to change. You'll be familiar with what's appropriate to your peers, partner, employer and culture, and how conventional or otherwise you want to be. A majority of men would probably prefer not to be noticed for their hair at all.

*Consider your face-shape and body-type.* Should you stick with a traditional barber or seek out a glitzy tonsorial artist? Paying a fortune isn't necessary, even for the well coiffed, except when you're considering a change and would welcome a stylist's advice.

• *Long hair suits those with prominent ears.* Today's long hair hangs no further than the collarbone, all-over long rather than layered, with no volume. Meanwhile it's modish for those with curly hair to give it some body.

• *Long hair may be inappropriate for your business,* and it's a nuisance when you're looking down. One solution is hair that hangs over the ears but not further than the lobes, extending to the collar at the back. With more volume, this can look good on older men. Mousse (such as Jason All Natural) may hold it gently in place. Leave hairspray to the ladies.

• *Shorter hair may look more sophisticated – and younger.* Go for short all over – not short at the sides and long on top – until the 1980s 'wedge' comes back!

• *Mid-length messy styles aren't natural by nature.* A paste or wax (Crew, KMS) is less crunchy than a gel (Clinique, Jason Hi-shine or Goldwell Definition). Apply after a wash and avoid combing your hair.

• *Traditional, parted haircuts* can be styled with pomades and brilliantine such as D. R. Harris (on London's St James Street), Trumper's Pomade, Brylcreem and Black & White. Some think Cecil Beaton, others Basil Fawlty.

# LOSING IT

Those with thinning hair may be inclined to think of restoration, however the fact that it's caused by androgen, the male hormone, suggests it can't be treated topically. Trying a product won't make it worse, but bear in mind that if your hair-loss stops, it may have done so in any case.

If you lose your hair, you have a new appearance to get used to, something not experienced since adolescence. Brushing your hair forward – the 'Roman Emperor' – suits some but may look like you're trying too hard to cover your brow. Gelled spikes, however, will accentuate your hair-loss.

Bear in mind that others will only see something as a shortcoming if you indicate that you do. Baldness is so common that people will naturally take in the things that make you an individual instead. If you wish, you can draw attention away from your head with facial hair or designer glasses.

## WASH YOUR HAIR IN A WAY THAT WON'T EXACERBATE HAIR LOSS:

•   Incline your head forward and use a detachable shower-head if possible, as if at a traditional barber.

•   Rinse thoroughly to remove dirt and dust.

•   Use as little shampoo as possible (unless you want your hair to be very full). Apply it evenly with both palms.

•   Massage it with your finger-ends, not the flat of your palms.

•   Rinse it through, preferably with cool or lukewarm water. One shampoo is usually enough.

•   Press water out of your hair with a hand towel – don't rub. If possible, dry your hair naturally.

*Recommended products to thicken hair*: Garnier white birch lotion, Shiseido Adenogen Hair Energizing Formula, Wella System Professional Just Men Maxximum Tonic (containing caffeine and menthol), together with the Gentle Shampoo in that range. Alternatively, eat food with low-fat proteins such as chicken and fish to help your hair stay strong.

# TIDY TEETH

In America, the appearance of one's teeth has long been an indication of status. This trend is slowly starting to make its way into Europe as more of us opt for cosmetic dentistry.

Good clothes and bad teeth is as dated a look, and as much a sign of ageing, as having a drab suit, greasy hair and glasses as thick as the bottoms of wine bottles. Unfortunately, many of the good things in life also stain them and for this reason an increasing number of people undertake the minor cosmetic (rather than remedial) dental option of tooth whitening.

Whitening can only lighten teeth to their original colour. Nonetheless, it can obscure the ravages of a lifetime caused by coffee, wine, tobacco and sugar. Some people may also have staining under the surface, thanks to tiny cracks that absorb matter, and discoloured teeth due to root-canal work, with which whitening gets results.

While there's a risk of error with home whitening kits, and many available in the UK contain a limited amount of hydrogen peroxide (the whitening agent), products such as Go Smile have established themselves in the US. For the full treatment, ask your dentist.

The first step involves a visit to the dentist for impressions to be taken for a mouth-guard. Gums are protected with gel or rubber while the whitening agent is applied from the guard. This treatment is continued at home for three to four weeks, or as little as one, since some agents can now be left on for longer at a time. Quicker still is laser or power whitening, in which a laser is shone onto the whitener to activate it.

If you brush regularly with a fluoride toothpaste, the effects of whitening can last for three years. Ideally you should brush your teeth in the morning and before you go to bed for two to three minutes. It's also important to floss, which will help keep your gums healthy.

# NAILS, HANDS & FEET

The thought of a manicure may seem unnecessary and perhaps even faintly ridiculous. There's dignity in labour, right? So a few bumps and broken nails just show you're honest and, well...handy. True, if your work is manual. For the rest of us who hit nothing harder than our computer keyboard, paying attention to our nails once a week will ensure we don't cut the palms of those we shake hands with!

## THE KIT:

*Cuticle pusher*
*Cuticle clipper*
*Nail clipper*
*Nail file/emery board*
*Buffer*
*Nailbrush*

• Have a bath, or soak the fingers in a bowl of soapy water.
• Push back your cuticles as far as is comfortable. They protect the nail bed so don't ravage them. Manicure kits contain steel pushers, but rosewood ones are more comfortable.
• Particles of cuticle that jut out, or 'quicks', can be removed with a cuticle clipper (with a wishbone-shaped blade that only meets at the end).
• If your nails are long, clip them across the top.
• Shape them with your file or emery board into a semi-circular shape. You can progress from a coarser to a finer file if it helps. Run your file briefly under the nail.
• If you wish, you can buff the edges of your nails with a buffer – much finer than a file, these are often found on the reverse side. Use a backwards-and-forwards motion (similar to brushing your shoes).
• Having a nailbrush on hand lets you remove dirt even when you're not going for the full manicure monty!

*A word about toes*: in contrast to your fingers, trim your toenails in a straight line across. File them if you wish, however it's best not to round them off because this can cause ingrown toenails.

# GROOMING KNOW-HOW

## OUR FRIENDS ELECTRIC

The range of electric shavers is bewildering. These days there are razors with up to two or three parallel foils (Remington, Braun), while Philishave's rotary blades are most common in threes but also seen in twos. First, decide whether you want to use a straight or rotary razor. Secondly, select your power option: mains, rechargeable or battery. Any decent shaver will also have a trimmer blade, and some are waterproof for easy cleaning and use in the shower.
***Recommended pre-electric shaves***: Aramis Classic or Anthony Electric Pre-Shave Solution for an effortless glide, especially if you've 'gone electric' to minimize shaving rash.

## REMEDIAL SOLUTIONS

If your skin is irritated, don't shave if you don't have to. Blunt blades can lead to ingrown beard hairs, so you should change them after about three uses. The skin reacts to an ingrown hair like it would any other foreign body and becomes sore. A hot compress may help eject the hair. Don't pick your skin, athough you may be able to extricate an especially large specimen with the tip of a toothpick before tweezing.
***Recommended products***: Tend Skin In-Growing Hair Solution and Air Shave Gel contain aspirin to calm skin irritations.

## SOFT HANDS

Even if your hands don't do dishes, make sure you give them a little TLC. Moisturizing will avoid tight, dry skin.

## THE HOLISTIC APPROACH

Tucking into junk foods won't help your skin. Saturated fats deposit toxic gunk, but mono-unsaturated fats (found in fish and cereal oils as Omega 3) are anti-inflammatory. Choose low-fat dairy options where possible. You should also eat foods that are low on the glycemic index, such as fruit, green vegetables and beans. Avoid treats that will give you a 'sugar rush'. And lastly, drink at least eight glasses of water a day. This will help keep your skin clear.

# Credits

**Thanks to the following companies for loan of props for photography**

**CHURCH'S**
201 Regent Street
London W1B 4NA
T: +44 (0)20 7734 2438

**DOORS BY JAS M. B.**
8 Ganton Street
London W1F 7QP
T: +44 (0)20 7494 2288
F: +44 (0)20 7494 2287
www.doorsbyjasmb.com

**DUNHILL**
www.dunhill.com

**GAP**
www.gap.com

**GEO. F. TRUMPER**
166 Fairbridge Road
London N19 3HT
T: +44 (0)20 7272 1765
www.trumpers.com

**GIEVES & HAWKES**
No.1 Savile Row
London W1S 3JR
T: +44 (0)20 7434 2001
F: +44 (0)20 7437 1092
www.gievesandhawkes.com

**JONES BOOTMAKER**
18 Maple Road
Eastbourne
East Sussex BN23 6NZ
www.jonesbootmaker.com

**LIBERTY**
Regent Street
London W1B 5AH
T: +44 020 7734 1234
F: +44 020 7573 9898
www.liberty.co.uk

**MARGARET HOWELL**
34 Wigmore Street
London W1U 2RS
T: +44 (0)20 7009 9006
www.margarethowell.co.uk

**MURDOCK**
340 Old Street
London EC1V 9DS
T: +44 (0)20 7729 2288
www.murdocklondon.com

**OLIVER SPENCER**
166 Fairbridge Road
London N19 3HT
T: +44 (0)20 7272 1765
www.oliverspencer.co.uk

**PINK**
**Thomas Pink**
Jermyn Street
London SW1Y 6JD
www.thomaspink.co.uk

**REISS**
www.reiss.co.uk

**TOPMAN**
www.topman.co.uk

# Acknowledgements

A special thank you to Murdock who allowed us to use their stylish premises for a day's photo shoot. The author would also like to thank Guy West of Jeffery-West for his footwear advice (www.jeffery-west.co.uk).

Endpapers image taken from *Weaving Patterns*, published by Pepin Press (www.pepinpress.com).